MEN_DONT_TALK

Quotes & Notes for Real People

Greg McBain

authorHOUSE®

AuthorHouse™
1663 Liberty Drive
Bloomington, IN 47403
www.authorhouse.com
Phone: 1 (800) 839-8640

Published by AuthorHouse 05/31/2017

ISBN: 978-1-5246-9464-7 (sc)
ISBN: 978-1-5246-9463-0 (e)

Print information available on the last page.

Any people depicted in stock imagery provided by Thinkstock are models,
and such images are being used for illustrative purposes only.
Certain stock imagery © Thinkstock.

This book is printed on acid-free paper.

Dedication

To all the people that have been in my life and are currently in my life, I have learned so much. Thank you all.

Contents

Acknowledgements... xi

Foreword.. xiii

Contact Information xv

Two Things 1

The Change Cycle 2

Inside You 3

Think and Do 4

Fearless... 5

Relationships 6

Complications 7

Addiction Success... 8

A True Heart... 9

Be 10

Procrastination 11

The Box.. 12

You are Beautiful... 13

Ultimate Success 14

Simplicity..15

Chaos...16

Doubt 17

People Pleasing..18

Fear...19

You.. 20

Perseverance 21

Struggle.. 22

Serenity.. 23

Life is Tough?... 24

Laziness... 26

Listening... 27

The Genesis of Motivation 28

Patience... 29

Happiness 30

Attitude of Gratitude...31

Strength 32

Wisdom 33

It's too hard.. 34

Think about it! 35

Focus 36

Progression.. 37

Start 38

Mondays Question.. 39

You know that…... 40

To know…... 41

Fundamental Rules for Success 42

Another Fear 43

1st Step to Positivity.. 44

Intentions...45

To Learn is to Succeed 46

Loving Yourself.. 47

IF 48

Intelligence... 49

You are Where You're Meant to Be........................ 50

Dance to Your Own Tune for Success

(Metaphor for Living) 51

If Motivation Wanes 52

Sleep 53

Negatives of Human Thinking............................... 54

2b..55

Someone You Love 56

There are… 57

Success 58

Decision 59

Mother 60

Be Successful...61

Successful Relationships................................. 62

Addictions.. 63

Focus 64

To have… 65

Evolutionary Revolutionary............................ 66

The Rat Race.. 67

FEAR (simplified) 68

Negative Association (Part 1) 69

Happiness 70

Have to 71

A brief chat….. 72

Pressure..74

Every time….. 75

How many…... 76

Simple Rules to Live By.................................. 77

Turmoil.. 78

Belief.. 79

Addiction is…... 80

Don't Know What I Want 81

Dances With Ghosts 82

Hard 84

Limits... 85

The Past 86

Success law.. 87

Want For Success 88

Waking up in Default Mode 89

Feelings, OMG You Say! 90

Predictable Unpredictability 91

Confidence isn't 92

If I could change the world 93

Someone Else's Success.. 94

Diagnosis… 95

Never Give up 96

If you can… 97

Looking back successfully 98

Accepting others... 99

As you reach… 100

Epilogue.. 101

Acknowledgements

To all of you who know what it takes to get where you need to go, you know who you are, thank you.

Foreword

All too often, we read a couple of words here and there, they sink in, in a two second epiphany, and bam were gone back to where we were before that, or trying to get what it meant because it's language either doesn't engage us or we can't understand it.

I wrote this book because I did realise that a lot don't understand what some 'quote' language is, and it shouldn't be reserved for those who are part of an educational system at all only. We live in a diverse world where methods of learning are not confined to a judicial system and the most important aspects of life are not thought on a curriculum like, self-awareness, motivation, etc. here in plain English I believe I try to explain it for the educated, non-educated etc. so that they may understand what it is everyone else is talking about. Spiritual and business language also is not understood by everyone so hopefully my intention was to simplify motivational success in all areas of living not just business or finance but personally too. Trust me there are superrich out there too who don't understand a lot of parts of normal life and vice versa. Hopefully my aim is to help you help yourself and spread the word and remember, life is simple, it's the person that is complicated.

Contact Information

Email; gmcbain.ecq@gmail.com
Facebook; Men_Dont_Talk
Instagram; Men_Dont_Talk
Twitter; @mendonttalk

Two Things

There are only 2 things in life that bother anyone.
That is 'What' they think of themselves
And what 'Others' think of them.

The Change Cycle

I cannot say I have truly changed,
Unless I have truly learned.
And I cannot say I have learned,
Unless I have truly understood.
And I cannot say I have understood,
Unless I am truly honest.
And I cannot say I am honest,
Unless I have truly listened.
And I cannot say I have listened,
Unless I have truly learned.
And I cannot say I have learned,
Unless I have truly changed.

Inside You

If you find heaven here on earth,
It is not a place, not a physical thing,
It is not an animal or religion,
Some Dare to even call it heaven,
For it is a popular belief.
But there is a bliss, a haven, a wonderful place that exceeds hate and wit and prayer.
It is a melancholy of its own with a microcosm of chaos that is this world that feels and dwells and nurtures homage to tearing down, by standing on their shoulders to feel tall.
For here in this realm is bliss and it can't be touched, if you know it well, it exists in 'your' spirit.
Ask the soul a question and your spirit will answer you, as the heart is both strong and weak.
You need this place to go to and it shall be where?
It shall be found where you least look and that is,
'Inside you'.

Think and Do

Thinkers do just that- 'Think'.
Do'ers do both – they think, but they do.
Successful people 'think', do, fail, try again.
Succeed.

Fearless

Fearless doesn't mean being, without fear.

It means being aware of it but you 'use it' to succeed in whatever you do.

Once you succeed, your fear will come, but your awareness with practice will succeed you to defeat them.

Relationships

A good relationship is like 2 great oaks,
in the busy forest.
Both need the light to survive.
Enough distance to grow all around so they don't block
each other's light and they both individually aspire towards
the light.
Deep beneath the soil they share the same resources and
unite.

Complications

Complications are only a justification of your limitations.

Addiction Success

A simplified explanation, taken from the book 'The Void' – G. McBain 2017.

Being sober is a bifold result of your reaction to life on your terms and life's terms' just being clean is NOT sober, that's just the physical part, you need to be sober spiritually and mentally also to be a success.

If you do not have the latter 2, the chances of you remaining sober are very slim.

You will just be a person whistling in the dark in a minefield, the latter brings you into the light so you can see where you are going, stronger and more successful which I will tell you how further in the book.

A True Heart

A true heart is rare, it is not a seeker nor does it rest.
It's deeper than the universe and transcends all other emotions with its strength. It's more trusting than fear, more selfless than ego, its gratitude never wants and it sacrifices all its own desires and wants for the true heart is not selfish. It doesn't care about looks. It cares not whether you love back or not.
It shines when even the darkness tries to kill it.

Be

Be the reason of someone else's inspiration.
You can only keep what you have by giving it away.

Procrastination

What's the definition of procrastination?
'I will tell you tomorrow'.

The Box

There's no such thing as the term
'Thinking outside the box'.
For successful people, there never was a box to start with
Just unlimited imagination and determination to succeed

You are Beautiful

The night ends with you,
The day starts with you,
You may meet many others,
Through the day that may,
Change your mind or,
The way you feel about you
But remember that there are 'Many' people but only
'One beautiful you'

Ultimate Success

Success is how you live.

Breathe, think and impact yourself and the world every day, it starts everyday with one foot out of the bed and on the floor early, no excuses, no matter how you feel, for the idea of success to become reality, you must learn success in all your moods,

You must change your thinking, vocabulary, and attitude.

If you dream of success only, that's all it is 'only a dream', do it now before someone else does, rise early, be you, and make it count, success is not money, not grandiosity, nor power, these are the by-products of success, real success is your personal victory in the making that dream a reality.

Simplicity

Life is simple.
It's the person that's complicated.

Chaos

Even in chaos there is order.
When there's an explosion, its ordered as it follows the rules of physics.
So even in life's chaos there is order, just train yourself to see it and understand it.
You gain this by personal awareness.
Success in chaos comes from 3 things:
Honesty, openness, willingness.
Learn your own shortcomings.
Master them and adapt.
No such word anymore as 'obstruction' only challenge and it all starts with 'you'.

Doubt

You will always doubt there's a god.
But you will never doubt there's a devil.
Self-doubt is the biggest sabotage in your life.
Self-belief only comes with practicing beyond your daily limits, if you stay comfortable you encourage fear.
If you push beyond the limits you create 'Yourself'.

People Pleasing

When you say' YES' to everyone else,
You are saying 'NO' to yourself.

Fear

Fear itself can't hurt you.

Fear is simply a negative rehearsal of the future. Learn to trust your pathway into the unknown, you can win success by working with fear, become its ally and do not run.

The sooner you befriend fear the more successful you will be.

You

No one else stops you from doing, but 'you'.
If you do nothing, that's 'you'.
If you do everything, that's 'you'.
Which 'you,' would you rather be?

Perseverance

The art of pushing through all your emotions towards success
The last step, take it.
The last push, push it.
The last metre, run it.
For the last of all these creates the new 'you'.

Struggle

Struggle is just a doorway to success.
Grip its handle and open it,
Because if it's dark inside always,
At least you get a third of it as light outside.
Which is easier?

Serenity

Only happens, not when you have banished negative emotions, but only when you have made allies of them and use them to your advantage.

Life is Tough?

Some say the that life is tough, it's hard and it's a melancholy that is unforgiving, it's a quagmire of frustrations and contempt's that we blame endlessly for making us unhappy, the daily ritual grind that is facetious and personifies absolute negativity. Most are not aware of the power they have, as your eyes open and your floodgates of negative impending thoughts thwart the very existence after your slumbering hours. The thought of the person place or thing that haunted your mind is eternal and never ceases. It waits for your eyes to open, for your vulnerable mind space to be invaded without your awareness. This my friends is where it needs to stop,

You take control back, it always was yours so why did you give it away, we live in a world where you must win everything, every argument (ego) every glancing eye or acknowledgement (attention), every task must be better than someone else's (insecurity), and "why", you may ask is within yourself. Why the need to prove? Why the need to be admired, adored, accoladed?

It's funny because we use negatives to gain all we look for to make us happy, some may see this as ying and yang, but if you never give your power away and hiss rather than bite like the swami tells us then you are half way there. If you do not need to win an argument, you've won,

If you don't need appraisal, you're content with how you are happiness is a by-product of good living, so make the most of it now, and if you want heaven here on earth, it is not a place not a physical thing, it is not an animal or religion, some dare to even call it heaven for it is a popular belief, but there is a bliss a haven a silent wonderful place that exceeds hate and wit and prayer.

It is a melancholy of its own with a microcosm of chaos that is this world, that feels and dwells and nurtures homage to tearing down others by standing on their shoulders to feel tall. For here in this realm is bliss, and u can't be touched if u know it well, it exists in your spirit. Ask the soul a question and the spirit shall answer you, as the heart is both strong and weak u need this place to go to and it shall be where?

It shall be found where u least look, and that is inside you.

Laziness

News! Laziness jailed for 1 year but risk of outbreak over murdering motivation.

Laziness lost the war today and was sentenced for crimes against mentality.

Among his comments were, but we don't feel well and I'm not able thus blackmailing his owner into bad health and way of living that depressed and was slowly killing his owner.

It was discovered by a good friend and coach, who immediately broke his cycle, and there were arguments etc, but persistence won out and laziness was arrested by surprise, he was subdued by body movement known to be laziness's weak spot. For now, we are glad to say he is under arrest and will remain dormant for sometime.

Moral is do 'you' want to put laziness in jail?

Listening

All communication begins with listening. It's amazing in today's world when we hear we only hear on the sound level, but listening is far more astute and acute that is taken for granted, that coupled with intuition and emotion involves listening to a whole new level. Some heard sounds but not the messages, some listen just for the moment as in just bearing it till the others voice is gone and then make judgements. A true empathiser hears and believes it or not listening to someone's voice, message and intention is a choice you make. If someone is prejudged then that person won't listen to them because either it tells truth, hurts or is cleverer than the listener who won't hear in revolt. Listening means connecting, hearing what is said, taking on board empathically what the underlying message may be and caring about what is being voiced.

We live in a world full of noise and it's not cerebral it's mental noise, frustrations, confusions, anger, lust, loathing and all of the above and more are distractions to the message. Many times a person will test you but there are only so many times till your voice gets weary and sense tells you it's no use the other isn't willing to communicate. Sad world really as most love the sound of their own voice when talking but they don't really listen, it's the silent ones that hear and feel the most and know that talk is not much good when it's not heard. If you can't listen then you can't really partake in another's life as you fail to understand them, you can't know their needs nor can you really know them as a person.

The Genesis of Motivation

The genesis of motivation arises from the pain of life realising how dormant and tired you have become of your current situation.

It's a 3-fold realisation (spiritual, physical, mental) of how stuck you have become.

You didn't see it creep up on you so don't blame yourself. Don't fret on the past or current, only focus on what you have and what you are willing to do about your problem or situation. Then make a choice. It will be fearful. It will be like a mountain. Easy way to start, wake up and put one leg on the floor, follow it by the other and move your body moving the body focuses the mind. Now if you can move your body, the world awaits your choices. Make the right ones. Learn to do it in all moods and make it a habit. A habit gets easier with practice thus motivation is born.

Patience

Many people while on the way to success suffer, humiliation, bewilderment, despair even the most successful. There are people who have everything yet wake up and feel lost because they lost themselves in the journey. Stay true and humble to yourself yet tough and realistic. Complications are only a justification of your limitations. In this world of instants 'Patience' is lost it is needed to quieten the mind, to reassess where you are at and rather than a crossroads think of it as a positive. People on destructive roads usually follow one road so you have crossroads, lucky you. Patience is a learning tool that most oversee, so think the next time you get this choice.

Happiness

Happiness is the bird that sings when the dawn is yet dark. Do not seek it for it is made, within you is all power to achieve contentment and wear it in your heart. Always strive for betterment and understanding, for the more you understand, the more you know you want. But become grateful for what you have also, and have not!

Attitude of Gratitude

If you have an attitude of gratitude you will gain all you need to succeed, be grateful for the negative person you just spoke to for you are not negative.

Be grateful for meeting the ill person for you are not sick.

Be grateful for the ignorant for you are aware.

Be grateful for the non-believers in life because you live.

Be grateful for the small minded because you are universal.

Now don't you realise there's a lot you 'haven't' got that you are grateful for, perfect reason to succeed.

Strength

You have strength you have not seen, all those troubles and situations you struggled through because someone else needs your help.

What if you saw yourself and could split in 2 what would you do to help 'You'.

Be honest and look hard.

While your helping you that is 'strength'.

Wisdom

The art of learning a new lesson

You failed so what?

You started again.

You learned.

So, you think you failed, I have news for you, you didn't, you gained.

You gained experience and the next time you try again is putting that experience into action, never let failure decide your fate, it's part of success, it builds strength, love for yourself, opens your eyes, exciting instead of debilitating.

The feeling is not wrong or right, bad or good it, just 'new' and you created it successfully from failure that's 'wisdom'.

It's too hard

If you think something is hard, congratulations, then you have reached a limit, it's your minds way of telling you we need help, more knowledge, more self-understanding, take it as a positive for your ego is saying it's too hard but your body and spirit is telling you show us more we can lean it so it's not hard anymore. Then you gain resilience, persistence, endurance, mentally and physically. So, the next time you think it's 'hard' that's just a positive to keep pushing forward, remember if your standing in life then you're already going backwards, you choose, turn 'herds' into 'easies' with practice.

Think about it!

If you don't put thought in tomorrow today, you will end up having done nothing yesterday.
Think about it!

Focus

Finding

Oneself

Constantly

Using

Self-discipline

Progression

Foolishness is noisy regression

While wisdom is silent progression

Start

To start something

You must stop

Stop thinking that is and just 'do'

Stop

Thinking

And

Reach

Target

Mondays Question

What part of 'You' are you going to challenge today?

Remember that fear is always there so get used to working with it, not run from it.

When you make fear your 'ally' you're a winner.

Move

Onward

Now

Direct

Action

Yields

Success

You know that...

You know that relationship 'you're' in where you're always told you're useless and you could never do it and these times when you always thought they were right so much you believed it. The days when you put everything off because it was too much trouble, the times when you laughed and your joy was short lived because they said you didn't deserve it. The way that they looked at you when you stood in front of a mirror and said 'nothing worth looking at, well its time you broke up, break of that relationship that sucks your life mentally, physically, spiritually. Yep that relationship you're in with 'yourself'.

Get a divorce as soon as possible and start listening successfully ok.

To know...

'To know the knowledge of the world is noble

But to know oneself is universal'

Fundamental Rules for Success

Get rid of the 'employee' mentality.

For successful people, there is no such thing as Monday to Friday week of work, if you're passionate about what you do, then it's not work.

Change your 'us' and 'them' employee view of life to the successful 'you' and the 'world' view.

Employees leave for work 10 mins before work starts and have a 15 min journey any wonder they are agitated all day after which hinders success. Successful people usually arrive an hour early because of their passion to succeed.

Employees like to blame others for mistakes.

Successful people take it on the chin and learn from it no matter how hard it is.

Family is no excuse for not being successful.

Plenty of Mothers/Dads succeed 'because' of their families either to give them a better life or wanting to be what their family 'wasn't'.

Another Fear

Fear of success is a truth for a lot of people.
For most it's not the fear of what's beyond,
It's just that they might not respond.

1st Step to Positivity

All too many times guru's and academics will use big words from the spiritual world and expect you to understand them, in plain English 'how' do you start being 'positive'

Move your body and by that I mean if you're in a rut, down or feeling bad you need to move, your head gets as big as the room you're in when static, your brain needs to coordinate the movement physically so you have to think about what you're doing, get up, wash dishes, clean a bit just move and get active preferably with close mouthed friend, someone and expose what's eating you. Remember you only have situations, 'not' problems. Train your situations by repeat taking control back, make decisions and decisions need action so you went from 'static' to literally moving 'forward' well done.

Intentions

Intentions put you on the road to hell, and by that, I mean you punish yourself for not doing, not starting etc.

Next time you get an intention the only way to make it happen is start getting honest with yourself and admit your intention to someone you know will push it, make a habit of 'committing' not 'intending'.

Intending is 'Always' past tense.

Committing is today and future.

Decide 'NOW'.

To Learn is to Succeed

Everything you have studied and memorised is great if you're into memory, but succeeding means breaking the parameters of everything you have learned and stretching it beyond its capacity to evolve into success. Otherwise remain the same as your fellow who got the same results. The reason you're not succeeding is because you are sticking to learned boundaries. All you learn in school or courses should never remain static once you receive a credit.

The reason you read or learn is because without success from others you would have a seriously hard time getting anywhere.

We only push limits till they are unlimited

To give someone else the tools to succeed, as well as ourselves, that's where you learn to be different.

Being different and maximising it makes you stand out and succeed.

Loving Yourself

The first things everyone wakes up to is the little voice box in your head, the one that has learned from all the negatives in life, the one that tells you look shit and quite frankly you listen don't you? Awareness is the key to breaking this, the world is not to be feared at all, it's you fearing yourself that blocks you off from the world to succeed. Become aware of the voice box in you and break it, you will never be rid of it but it needs educating from you and others. The voice box you currently have is charged with the murder of motivation, con job the voice box until it gets real by getting your body to do the opposite of those negatives. It will be reaffirmed after in self-confidence, self-assurance etc.

Key is, get self-awareness first and know who you are fearlessly, flaws too, for you.

Cannot change, what you cannot see or not aware of, start there.

IF

IF stands for 'Inevitably Fucked'.
Remove the If's from your life and replace with 'DID',
Doing Inspire of Defeat.

Intelligence

The fact that you have many qualifications etc. doesn't make you intelligent, it proves you can memorise stuff that's all. It does so you can sit in a back office somewhere and never be heard of till break time. IQ is fine when you're in an inspired mood or feeling good, that's fine but the winner in all life and success is emotional intelligence. It underlies IQ and if mastered then it boosts your IQ inevitably. It's what holds you up in all moods emotions, pressure etc. You cannot gain EI unless you are fully aware of yourself and how you tick. It's not looking for flaws only strengthening them so you have a good foundation for IQ. Remember IQ is not much use if you can't deal with everyday reactions to life.

Motivation comes from how you handle life regardless of how much you think you know from textbooks etc. Master yourself to begin with or as you go rather than memorise, anyone can memorise but not everyone can master EI (Emotional Intelligence).

You are Where You're Meant to Be

This is another way of someone saying shut the F'up. Reality is you are where you are because you either react badly or didn't react at all to the life you were dealt primarily but in the end, you made yourself. All is not lost because you were unaware of how you got there but now reading this you are aware and you need to become more aware to move forward, coupled with fear and knowledge. True friends and colleagues will never say you're meant to be where you are. Learn the world after learning yourself and make where you are, of YOUR MAKING.

Dance to Your Own Tune for Success (Metaphor for Living)

You may not have invented notes or instruments but you can learn to play them well and create your own masterpiece. Let it be you, your business or your life. You may go from metal to classical in life, learn from all genres and do yourself a favour.

Before you make your mind up,

'Open it'.

If Motivation Wanes

1. Learn what times you're most productive and when you love doing what you do.
2. If you're lacking, help another person toward success it reignites your own passion.
3. Do what you least like first like delayed gratification that way there's a payoff on the last task of day.
4. Break old habits it stimulates body and mind, alter the way you wake up, spend evenings etc.
5. Accomplish short-term goals.
6. Ease pressure as this leads to frustration and that leads to resentment of what you're trying to achieve, step back and breath, refocus.

Develop your emotional intelligence so your emotions don't demotivate you.

That comes from learning self- awareness.

Sleep

Almost all motivated successful people find that sleep while essential, gets in the way of progress. Fact is most successful people only get between 4-5 hours' sleep per night not because they are worried but because they have passion.

If you love what you do it's not work.

If you find yourself working, then you're doing the wrong thing for you.

Be fearless and follow your passion.

Negatives of Human Thinking

To assume a negative label given to you by the worlds professions and you accept it is to assume the role of a victim.

'He/she suffers from' is no excuse for lack of brainpower or achieving success unless it is physically damaged it can be justified.

'My --- doesn't let me do this or do that,'

Means your view is narrowed by your self-labelling. Therefore you define yourself as limited, then you 'are' limited. Ask Stephen Hawking if he labels himself in anyway?

Moral is 'YOU'. Accept other's definitions of yourself. 'STOP'. Start by defining 'YOURSELF' and create 'WHO' you are that is successful. This is done with fear, insecurity etc. but with practice and help from other winners you can be who you really want to be.

2b

2b or not 2b!!!
To a successful person is just a pencil!

Someone You Love

Having someone you love, it's about having someone who is willing to walk through the hard times with you. It's about having someone who sees all the beauty inside of you that everyone else overlooked. The goal when it comes to love should never be about finding someone who is perfect. The goal should always be to find someone who is worth it. If you already know that you are not a finished product, why are you expecting someone else to be? Find someone who you can go through healthy progressions with without giving you a headache. Find someone who has a healthy heart. Someone who won't allow their pains from the past to influence how they treat you. Someone family oriented building towards the future. Someone who isn't afraid to dream too big. Someone you can have fun with but also enjoy peace and quiet with. Love is so beautiful when you know it makes sense to have a certain person in your life.

There are...

There are only 2 things in life that bother anyone.
That is, what they think of themselves and what others think of them.

Success

Success is
Making obstacles into challenges,
It builds character,
Temperance and knowledge

Decision

If you decide not to
decide to do something
that in itself is a decision.

Mother

You can only have one mother
Patient, kind, and true
No other friend in all the world
Will be the same as you
When other friends forsake you
To mother you will return
For all her loving kindness
She asks nothing in return
As we look upon her picture
Sweet memories will recall
Of a face, so full of sunshine
And a smile for one and all

Be Successful

Be successful like a bird taking off,
He trusts in what he can't see,
Yet he jumps and opens his wings.
His faith in himself makes him sing while the dawn is still
dark
Because like the sun is real.

Successful Relationships

Communication
If both partners were mind readers, neither would be together as one would be working in a circus.
So, honest talking, not expecting a partner to guess or assume is vital to knowing one another's needs.

Addictions

Willpower has the same effect on addiction
as it has on stopping diarrhoea.
Try it and see!

Focus

If you don't focus
On where you're
Going.
You're likely to end
up where you're
Heading.

To have...

To have true power
You must first admit that you have none
Then everything is achievable

Evolutionary Revolutionary

In order to gain success personally you must break the apron strings and balls and chains of past. Apron strings mean depending on others for your security, balls and chains are insecurity, past problems, past values, past ideals, most of the latter are under one heading - 'FEAR'. Yep they are all variations of fear from the KPI manager who rules because he lacks control, to the employee who goes to work thinking the world owes him something.

The world owes you 'nothing'. Same as the ocean, the fish are not going to get out of the water and knock on your door. Why would they? In order to succeed you must be a leader not a control freak with issues and make new roads for others to follow. Create a path 'With' fear and you shall gain courage. Drop the old thinking and elevate to new ways in current times. People are still moulded by parameters of old time psychology from men who existed over 50 years ago, who have no idea about today. 'Why?' because they're dead. Wake up and smell the roses from this season, not last century and grab the world because truth is, it certainly won't knock on your door anytime soon.

It's up to you to grab it, run with it, be a winner and make others winners too.

The Rat Race

Man, has no 'Problems' whatsoever. They are all but situations, they come they go, situations are temporary. The positive side of this is that you 'do' need to be tested all the time to ascertain what strengths have weakened and vice versa as well as showing your new needs to succeed. Don't be a monk who can only survive with other monks, living in the past, or the hermit in the hills seeking silence. The true successful person is in society with all its temporary flaws, people and places. There you succeed, not because you're having a problem with it but because you are embracing it, learning how it works and soon you can be the one who helps change it, become self-aware, strengthen it, be led by it, even with fear, and lead from it so others benefit.

FEAR (simplified)

Finding
Emotional
Acceptance
Real

There is a stigma out there that fear is bad.

Only mankind could label this, wild not domesticated animals treat fear the same as every other tool they have for survival.

FEAR is neither bad nor good so you need to eradicate this dichotomy out of your life.

Look at it as an aid, like a wise old person its telling you something, it means you need to learn is all, and fear is actually guiding you to overcome 'yes' overcome.

The reason it feels intense is, because if it were easy you wouldn't bother and degenerate into nothingness, mentally, spiritually and physically. See Fear as your older siblings kicking your ass 'why' because they love you.

Fear is, simply the universe's way of nudging you forward. It protects when you cross roads, stands at heights, depths etc. It protects you positively so why wouldn't it protect you when you're trying to succeed? Yes, you are afraid. Yes you want. Notice how 'want 'and 'fear' are always hanging around together as they always will. 'We' are the ones who see fear as negative instead of positive.

Negative Association (Part 1)

Believe it or not we are trained by our past, our bosses of old our mates, our relationships, but underneath all this is a blueprint of you that has become shrouded in a quagmire of dust and dirt. Filters are blocked hence no more reasoning, and the funny thing is, is that no matter how far down a person gets they can still look down.

Whoever said that humans should keep looking down? Emmm you were trained to, conditioned too. Understand that and your eyes level off, now you can see ahead. 'Yes' be aware of looking down but smile at it. Now break those associations and negative thoughts by replacement, change your view. If you didn't like Mondays then find something good about it. Mondays never did anything to you. They are the same always so it's 'you' that needs to change. After practice you go from looking straight across to metaphorically up because you're not looking down anymore. 'Yes' remember the 'old' you is always there so be careful. Learn this fact and as soon as you accept it that fear will 'always' be there then it will be much easier. So start 'Now'. I don't care what you're doing, do it now.

He who puts it off, puts off success.

Happiness

You cannot find it
You cannot search for it
You cannot buy it
You cannot expect it
You cannot hope for it
You cannot pray for it
You cannot seek it
Happiness is a 'by- product of living well
Start there and instead of you looking for it
'It finds you'

Have to

I have to lift this. I have to finish that. I have to do this and I have to do that to succeed. Stop right there because with that mode of thinking you're going to lose. Yes lose or create more work for yourself.

You need to 'want' to lift it, finish it etc. to succeed. Simple self-awareness of how you talk to yourself changes everything.

Change 'have' to into 'want' to otherwise don't do it at all.

A brief chat...

A brief chat to the one, your other half who doubts you
inside- YOU
You never say you need me,
You never say you want me,
You never say I miss you,
That way that I miss you,
You never say u want to kiss me,
You never say you will hug me,
You never say I adore you,
That way that I adore you,
You never say its ok,
You never say don't worry,
You never say that I'm here for you,
That way I am for you,
You never say hold my hand,
You never say take a stand,
You never say be gentle,
The way I am with you,

You never say I'm lonely,
You never say I'm excited,
You never say I can't wait,
That way I can't wait with you.
You never say I'm touched,
You never say I'm happy,
You never say you're amazing,
That way I am with you,

You never say the words, that make a heart feel near,
You never show emotions for all that you fear,
You then will never love because of your protected heart,
And every night you will cry because love didn't even start,
And only when it's gone you realise just how much,
All those words you never said would have meant so much,
And you wonder why I'm gone
And didn't seem to care
Cause all those words I said to you always when I was there
So, I took the silence you gave me,

it was empty without words,
And silenced myself from your heart
So, that mine will not be heard.
'Love yourself first'.

Pressure

Pure
Resistant
Emotion
Suffocating
Self
U
Rise
Emotionally

Pressure is the gym for your mental, spiritual, physical wellbeing. Go regularly and learn techniques to master it for the greater it gets you know you CAN handle it.

Every time...

Every time you drop your head
Make sure you're walking forward
Every time you take an ear bashing
Make sure you're moving forward
Every time someone takes strips of you
Make sure you're walking forward
Every time you have no money
Make sure you're walking forward
Every time you feel like shit
Keep walking forward
Every time you feel alone
Keep walking forward
Every time you think its futile
Keep walking forward
For every time, you're walking forward
You are never quitting just heading toward success. You're
not being beaten by life; you are being moulded for success

How many...

How many 'I's' do you see in fear
How many 'I's' do you see in can't
How many 'I's' do you see in not able to
How many I's' do you see in defeat
There's none because 'I' can do it

Simple Rules to Live By

Listen only to winners. There's quality of life determines whether you take their advice or not otherwise don't listen.

Forget what your parents said. Negatively it's not their fault, they are from the past, and you are about the future.

Don't fall into emotional traps of friend's, partners etc. If life needs to change you must have the courage to do it, hurt as few as you can, that's reality.

If you have to think twice about problems, make your own decisions. You can only learn by trial and error, error later becomes experience so you win.

Change the way you talk to yourself.

This must be done as soon as you open your eyes in the morning, make it a habit in all moods.

Learn to change no matter what mood you're in as you need to take control back mentally, not let your mentality control you.

Do it now.

Turmoil

The reason you're most likely turmoil is because you have 20th century fox channel in your head. You have the lead role in every movie for which you should win an Oscar because it is in their uncontrolled drama arises. It's not based on really what's going to happen so your mind is free from reality and has the power to intensify it till you freeze from the real world. To end turmoil you need to stop the movie snowballing out of control, bring each ailment out into the light by acknowledging it; formulate a solution to deal with it. A solution means a decision, which implies action. Action is the art of moving forward, despite fear and failure. Rewrite your script but make sure it's a successful ending.

Belief

All denominations, doctrines, programs, philosophies, psychologies, sects, religions are all based on one commonality.

Nothing to do with conscious or subconscious, gods or goddesses, leaders, presidents, or authority, even the mysterious Melchizedek, and that is what every individual has, 'every individual'.

It is called 'belief'. How powerful you make it is up to you and defined by the parameters you allow yourself to live in. Forget all the doctrines for today and start believing in 'yourself' to succeed. You are the universe, endless, as you want to be. So start living today in a way that is successful to you and benefits all people. You can't do that until you become self-aware first then you gain power for success.

Addiction is...

Addiction is the greatest love affair in your life. It will love you to death, will be your one and only partner and remove everything you have that is either useful or gets in the way. It's the only disease that will tell you 'you haven't got it'. That's how powerful it is. Every emotion you have is governed by it. It will get you to the point where you will only be doing 3 things, you will either be suffering from it, obsessed about the next time you have it or actually doing it. Then if you're lucky that leaves you with only 3 choices and that is abstinence, the Asylum or the morgue. That simple.

Don't Know What I Want

Until you do know don't be afraid to try everything that you even don't know. If in doubt stay where you're at till the pain motivates you to change. You may have to do this many times but don't lose heart. It's just the universe's way of getting you more experience toward your ultimate destination.

The journey is just as important as the goal.

The journey teaches you about fear and how to overcome it. It teaches your strengths, weaknesses, skills, it also teaches you 'who' to have around you. Remember those cans that make the most noise are people with no experience and are just fear projectors. Not you though you go for it, learn and win. Most successful people never reach one goal, they reach many hence; not knowing what you want is the greatest lesson of life.

Dances With Ghosts

You dance with ghosts, and all of the time,
They follow you everywhere and in your ears, they rhyme,
And tell you to dance and follow their tune,
Take you out of reality and do so till noon,
You cry as they waltz and stuck in their grip,
You turn your head but quiver your lip.
They demand you to dance, even when you're afraid,
And keep you awake from the dreams you have made.
They tire you out and laugh in your face
While you scream, and plead they spin you with grace.
The tune never ends while you write the next verse.
And the ghosts will dictate, as with you they rehearse,
The very next dance and the way you will flow
Your ghosts want you near and never let go.
As you tire and scream and want for the door,
The ghosts keep you dancing and waltz you some more.
And it spirals and spirals and nostalgia is now pain,
They won't let you go, forever again.
For the only way, out is to set them all free,
The ghosts your music created are always with thee.
So, silence the music and change the score,
Fill dancing with laughter and a smile to the fore.
Forgive the ghosts for they did not, have you,
It was you who had them and they waltzed with you.
How easy was pain when you dance with the ghost?
All your life being a dancer, and it was the host.
Now dance in the sun and set those ghosts free,

You write your own music any genre it can be.
For a waltz with the ghosts you banish with sun,
And fear pain no more and never run.
The music you will hear will rhyme in your ears,
And set you so free, and banish your fears.
So, you dance with a joy and someone you love,
And open the shutters and in light from above.

Hard

If something you're doing is painfully hard, as in not giving
you gains in life, only diminishing you
Then
Halt
And
Reassess
Direction

Limits

LIMITS are to be seen as positive

They are your new teacher every time you reach them. Those who don't reach limits are just existing and not moving forward.

Limits bring fear also but this is just a signpost to lead you in the right direction.

If it's not hard it's not worth doing.

If you don't learn from limits and fear or meet the challenge you are insulting your own quotient both intellectually and emotionally.

Labelled

Insecurities

Making

Insecure

Thoughts

Successful

The Past

The past exists only in memory, consequences and effects; it has power over you only as you freely give it power. Release it to move forward freely. You are not your past so success is free of chains that hold you down. If part of success is getting help to free you from your past then that in itself is success, for acknowledging weakness and facing it is strength.

Success law

Learn
Adapt
Win

Ask yourself this question:

There's shit in your life, you're always worried, you carry stress or make it and it's not yours. All the dickheads you know are over 18 and legally responsible for themselves, none of them are asylum certified, then why the F' are you carrying 'their' negatives that hinder 'your' success

It's Time the duty you bore for others, is laid upon yourself. Stop being responsible for over 18's and stop being a martyr. While others are quite comfortable standing on your shoulders, you hinder their lessons in life.

Let this be 'your' lesson and start by taking your own life back and make it successful, don't drag others, led by example and they will follow because they learned.

Want For Success

Most give up because they feel they have the old shitty life to fall back on, which doesn't look so bad when treading fear going into the unknown; hence, if we give up it makes no difference. Being the same old shit is easier than succeeding etc. Become aware and change that view. Imagine there is nothing to go back to, that you must make changing into you wanting and needing to make it. Anyone with a backup plan has already told themselves they are not going to make it, for they are already starting off with the failure side. It's subconscious failure that needs to go, if there is no back up plan that is all the motivation you need to succeed.

Waking up in Default Mode

Most people wake up in a default mode, hence having non-morning types etc. It's the way we have conditioned ourselves or our living environment has trained us to be, unknowingly or unwittingly. Some wake in defensive mode, others in neutral, but both are vulnerable, as when waking is when your most susceptible to negatives etc. You need to become aware and change it to succeed. Others who live with you may not comply but with practice you train yourself to see positively with gratitude, it will become a habit eventually and default-waking mode. As you set your scene for the days goals, remember positivity is the best defence for shitty mornings, your choice always.

Feelings, OMG You Say!

Yes the dreaded 'F' word revered by many, as you read this I guarantee you are feeling right this minute, whether induced by Monday or someone or something. Of course most just want the good feeling but you learn most from the negative ones, not 'bad' but negative. You choose to call it bad, stop that kind of thinking. You cannot change feeling directly but you can change thinking and as a result, your feelings change. Look upon negative feelings as signposts, they either warn you while on the way to success or reward you for how you are dealing with life.

Change the way you look at feelings, learn to stand back and chose by touching in with them. All feelings usually give you a message that you need to correctly listen to, then you decide by thought which action to take. That is success. Become self-aware of how you tick and then make a success instead of an emotional bomb.

Predictable Unpredictability

You wake up everyday doing the same routine same habits, drive to work the same way, listen to the same people, do the same grind, do the same drive home, same evening and it all leads to daydreaming. Fine if you're going to be the next great novelist or next big moviemaker but even they are unpredictable and that's what creates opportunity. How can you expect to succeed if you don't create opportunity? So if you're doing the same things everyday and it works that's fine but for hungry people boredom sets in, you need higher goals. Change how you go to work change what doesn't produce opportunity. You need new fears not old ones, you need to shed skin all the time so you renew and renewing can be created from changing what doesn't work into finding what does work. Just be brave enough to change mundane into insane success, or else carry on dreaming. Success in your head is futile without follow through. If you're at work or no matter where you are right now change one thing about the rest of today and see how you feel. 'Alive' is my bet. Go on what are you waiting for.

Confidence isn't ...

Confidence isn't
Being in people's faces having to get your point across
Controlling everyone and everything around you
Knowing everything that's going on when you don't need to
Having to win every argument
Having the last say in a discussion or meeting
Telling your partner how to live
Always plugging how great you are
How you make everyone think you're fearless
How you are the centre of everyone's universe and the list goes on, these are all traits of insecurity and fear and the need for control.

The successful, confident person doesn't need approval for they know where they are going. They don't argue because to enter the debate you lose. They save their words for more useful life success and they'd rather be followed by a partner or team than control them, that's true confidence. It is a silent master of his own emotions without broadcasting it or needing an audience. All the rest are just loud whistlers in the dark.

Start on your own self-awareness today and build your confidence silently but potently.

If I could change the world

Well you will if you change the way you talk.

'If I could' is always daydreamers speak and remains so. Others take it a step further. How you might ask? Simple, they change their vocabulary and replace with more powerful active words. Now change the first sentence again starting with putting in 'I Will' instead of 'IF I could' then that implies, how you are going to do it and what emotions it churns up

The words you use talking to yourself are very important to actually achieving desired outcome. Use active words instead of dreamer words; it pulls the dream into reality.

Someone Else's Success

If you are working on someone else's success, I have news for you. There isn't much planned for 'your' success in there so you need to work on your own successes. Start now, no excuses. Start with 'you'. Are you worth it? Put all that effort you give into others into succeeding yourself.

Diagnosis...

Diagnosis; Motivation
Prognosis; Success
Try diagnosing yourself as successful rather than all the negatives you usually do. I would rather have the troubles of success than suffering from negative diagnosis we give ourselves from our own involvement in life.

Never Give up

To want to be successful you cannot even try to understand the alternative to success. It is not an option so don't make it so. Success is seeking what you know is seeking you ultimately. It defies logic. There is no timing, no right time, tons of fails and disappointments. Don't settle for less because less will settle for you. Aim high and win the game you set out to do. Beat the rules. Reinvent everything and create success that is based on you.

Never Give up.

If you can...

If you can master fear within you than no fear outside can harm you.

Looking back successfully

For a successful person, looking backwards is a lesson not a regret, for you see how far you have come but also every person you dealt with didn't weaken you but helped you make 'you' stronger and more determined.

Accepting others

If you already know that you are not a finished product why are you expecting someone else to be? But do strive to help them finish themselves successfully.

As you reach...

As you reach toward success remember, not everyone is going to like you. The sooner you accept that the better. Like yourself first, then it doesn't matter who does or doesn't after.

Epilogue

In the twilight of dawns Dew
Came a taint of light
Whether divine or not, a Glimpse, a shred of minute hope,
which I clung so desperately too having faith in it to stop
this hell,
Like being reborn, a new spirit tainted in a battered shell,
that suffered from the unknown dogs of fear, ravaging out
from within, ageing me. But it is the pain of rebirth.
From the experience that made recovery possible and the
faith is the struggle, not just to bear but how better I become
by it.

Printed in the United States
By Bookmasters